JACK and Jill

Flip-Side Rhymes

From the perspective of JACK

by Christopher Harbo
illustrated by Colin Jack

PICTURE WINDOW BOOKS
a capstone imprint

Jack and

Jill

went up the hill

4

to fetch
a pail
of water.

Jack fell down
and broke his crown,

and Jill came tumbling after.

10

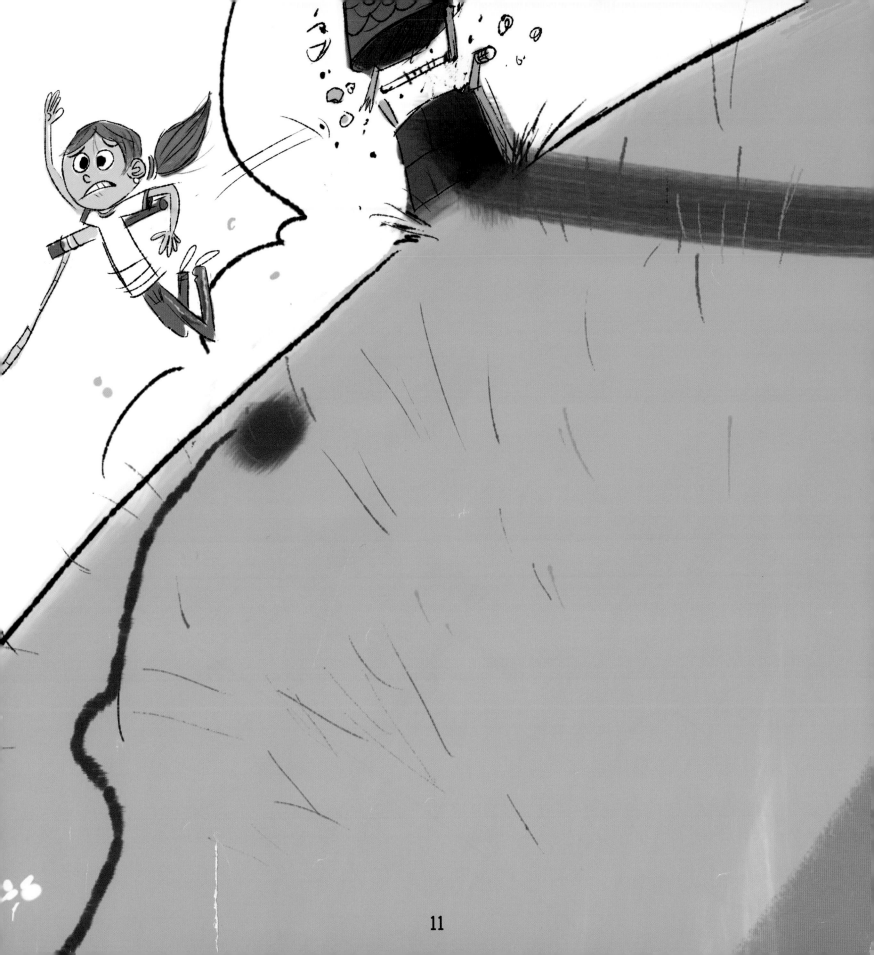

NOW FLIP THE BOOK
TO GET ANOTHER SIDE OF THE RHYME.

Picture Window Books are published by Capstone.
1710 Roe Crest Drive, North Mankato, Minnesota 56003
www.capstonepub.com

Library of Congress Cataloging-in-Publication Data
Harbo. Christopher L.
  Jack and Jill flip-side rhymes / by Christopher Harbo : illustrated by Colin Jack.
     pages cm. — (Nonfiction picture books. Flip-side nursery rhymes)
  Summary: "Color illustrations and simple text give the original Jack and Jill
nursery rhyme. along with a fractured version from the perspective of Jill"—
Provided by publisher.
  ISBN 978-1-4795-5988-6 (library binding)
  ISBN 978-1-4795-5992-3 (paperback)
  ISBN 978-1-4795-6004-2 (big book)
  ISBN 978-1-4795-6008-0 (paper over board)
  ISBN: 978-1-4795-6986-1 (ebook PDF)
  1. Nursery rhymes. 2. Children's poetry. 3. Upside-down
books—Specimens. [1. Nursery rhymes. 2. Upside-down books.]
  I. Jack. Colin. illustrator. II. Mother Goose. III. Title.
   PZ8.3.H19669Jac 2015
   398.2—dc23 [E]   2014032213

Editor: Gillia Olson
Designer: Ashlee Suker
Art Director: Nathan Gassman
Production Specialist: Laura Manthe
The illustrations in this book were created digitally.

Printed in the United States of America in North Mankato. Minnesota.
092014   008482CGS15

NOW FLIP THE BOOK
TO GET ANOTHER SIDE OF THE RHYME.

Internet Sites

FactHound offers a safe, fun way to find Internet sites related to this book. All of the sites on FactHound have been researched by our staff.

Here's all you do:

Visit *www.facthound.com*

Type in this code: 9781479559886

other titles in this series:

Humpty DUMPTY
Flip-Side Rhymes

Little **BO PEEP**
Flip-Side Rhymes

Little **MUFFET**
Miss
Flip-Side Rhymes

crowns sport stitches!

Now both their

Her laces caught on the
pail he brought.

so she kicked him
in the britches.

as they climbed the hill,

Jack shoved Jill

JACK and Jill

FLIP-SIDE RHYMES

From the perspective of Jill

by Christopher Harbo

illustrated by Colin Jack

PICTURE WINDOW BOOKS
a capstone imprint